LADY GAGA

FAMOUS ENTERTAINER

WITHDRAWN

KATIE LAJINESS

Big Buddy Books
An Imprint of Abdo Publishing
abdopublishing.com

BIG
BUDDY POP BIOGRAPHIES

abdopublishing.com

Published by Abdo Publishing, a division of ABDO, PO Box 398166, Minneapolis, Minnesota 55439.
Copyright © 2018 by Abdo Consulting Group, Inc. International copyrights reserved in all countries.
No part of this book may be reproduced in any form without written permission from the publisher.
Big Buddy Books™ is a trademark and logo of Abdo Publishing.

Printed in the United States of America, North Mankato, Minnesota.
052017
092017

THIS BOOK CONTAINS
RECYCLED MATERIALS

Cover Photo: Richard Shotwell/Invision/AP.
Interior Photos: Andy Kropa/Invision/AP (p. 6); ASSOCIATED PRESS (pp. 15, 23); Chris Pizzello/Invision/
    AP (p. 19); Everett Collection/Shutterstock.com (p. 23); ©iStockphoto.com (p. 9); Jason Squires/
    Contributor/Getty (p. 13); Jonathan Short/Invision/AP (p. 5); Jordan Strauss/Invision/AP (p. 21);
    Kevin Mazur/Contributor/Getty (p. 25); Matt Sayles/Invision/AP (p. 29); Mim Friday/Alamy Stock
    Photo (p. 23); REUTERS/Alamy Stock Photo (pp. 17, 19); Sipa USA via AP (p. 27); Theo Wargo/
    Staff/Getty (p. 11); Tinseltown/Shutterstock.com (p. 23); Veronica S. Ibarra/Contributor/Getty
    (p. 11); ZUMA Press, Inc./Alamy Stock Photo (p. 13).

Coordinating Series Editor: Tamara L. Britton
Graphic Design: Jenny Christensen

Publisher's Cataloging-in-Publication Data

Names: Lajiness, Katie, author.
Title: Lady Gaga / by Katie Lajiness.
Description: Minneapolis, MN : Abdo Publishing, 2018. | Series: Big buddy
    pop biographies | Includes bibliographical references and index.
Identifiers: LCCN 2016962361 | ISBN 9781532110610 (lib. bdg.) |
    ISBN 9781680788464 (ebook)
Subjects: LCSH: Lady Gaga--Juvenile literature. | Singers--United States--
    Biography--Juvenile literature.
Classification: DDC 782.42164092 [B]--dc23
LC record available at http://lccn.loc.gov/2016962361

CONTENTS

MOTHER MONSTER

Lady Gaga is a famous singer and songwriter. She is an **award**-winning artist whose fans call her Mother Monster. Her fans are known as Little Monsters.

A fashion icon, Lady Gaga has a creative sense of style. She has appeared on TV and in magazines.

NAME:
Stefani Joanne Angelina
"Lady Gaga" Germanotta

BIRTHDAY:
March 28, 1986

BIRTHPLACE:
New York City, New York

POPULAR ALBUMS:
The Fame, The Fame Monster,
Born This Way, ARTPOP, Joanne

FAMILY TIES

Stefani Joanne Angelina Germanotta was born on March 28, 1986, in New York City, New York. Her parents are Joseph and Cynthia Germanotta. She has a younger sister named Natali.

When Stefani was growing up, her father had an internet business. Her mother worked in an office.

WHERE IN THE WORLD?

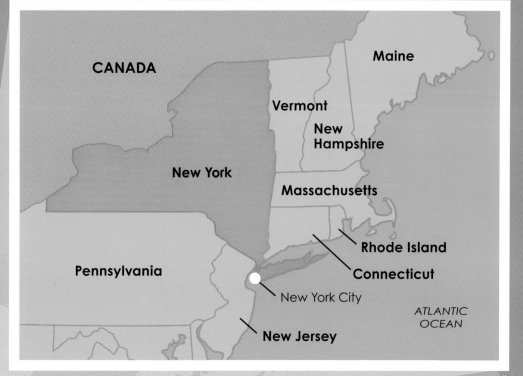

CANADA

Maine

Vermont

New Hampshire

New York

Massachusetts

Pennsylvania

Rhode Island

Connecticut

New York City

New Jersey

ATLANTIC OCEAN

EARLY YEARS

From a young age, Stefani loved music. When she was four, she learned to play the piano. At 13, she began writing songs.

In school, Stefani tried out for plays. She often won the lead **role**. At 17, Stefani went to college. But, she dreamed of becoming a **pop** star. So, Stefani left college after one year.

Stefani attended New York University's Tisch School of the Arts.

RISING STAR

Stefani worked hard to make her dream come true. She began to **perform** at small clubs around New York City. As part of her act, she used the stage name Lady Gaga.

In 2005, Lady Gaga signed a contract with a record label. Three months later, the company dropped her. But Lady Gaga refused to give up.

Growing up, Lady Gaga felt misunderstood by her peers. So, music was a way to express herself.

In 2007, Lady Gaga began working as a songwriter. She wrote songs for **pop** stars such as Britney Spears and Fergie. Then a **producer** discovered Lady Gaga. Soon, she had a new record deal.

Lady Gaga worked hard to write her own songs. In 2008, she **released** her first album, *The Fame*. The album was a hit! Lady Gaga's first single, "Just Dance," was **nominated** for a **Grammy Award**.

DID YOU KNOW
Lady Gaga wrote "Just Dance" in ten minutes!

Lady Gaga sang at the 2007 Lollapalooza music festival in Chicago, Illinois.

In 2008, Lady Gaga performed at a Jingle Ball concert in New York City.

A POP STAR'S LIFE

Lady Gaga's dream had come true. She had become a **pop** star. In 2011, she **released** her second album, *Born This Way*. It included hit songs "Yoü and I" and "Born This Way."

By this time, Lady Gaga had fans around the world. In 2013, she named her third album *ARTPOP*. Sadly, this album was not as successful as the others. But Lady Gaga continued to **perform** and write music.

In 2011, Lady Gaga met fans in Taichung City, Taiwan. The city's mayor declared July 3 Lady Gaga Day.

As a talented **performer**, Lady Gaga wanted to sing different kinds of music. So, she sang with **jazz** singer Tony Bennett. In 2014, they made an album called *Cheek to Cheek*.

Lady Gaga's success continued with her 2016 album, *Joanne*. This album mixed different sounds such as country, **pop**, and rock music.

In 2015, Lady Gaga and Tony Bennett sang "Cheek to Cheek" at the Grammy Awards.

AWARD SHOWS

At **award** shows, Lady Gaga often appears as a **performer** and a **nominee**. At the 2015 **Academy Awards**, she sang songs from *The Sound of Music*.

The next year, Lady Gaga sang "Million Reasons" at the **American Music Awards**. She has also won many awards for her music. As of 2016, Lady Gaga has taken home six **Grammy Awards**.

In 2015, Lady Gaga and Tony Bennett won Grammy Awards for Best Traditional Pop Vocal Album for *Cheek to Cheek*.

Lady Gaga sang "Till It Happens to You" at the 2016 Academy Awards.

ACTING CAREER

Lady Gaga always wanted to be an actress. In 2012, she was a voice actor on *The Simpsons*. Two years later, Lady Gaga appeared in the *Muppets Most Wanted*.

In 2015, Lady Gaga appeared in a TV series called *American Horror Story: Hotel*. The next year, she won a **Golden Globe Award** for this **role**.

During her Golden Globe acceptance speech, Lady Gaga said winning the award was one of the greatest moments of her life.

FASHION ICON

Lady Gaga is very confident about her sense of style. She wears fun outfits to express her personality. Sometimes, she wears wigs or dyes her hair for a new look.

She also appears in **advertisements** for fashion lines. These photos usually appear in magazines and on billboards.

DID YOU KNOW?
In 2010, Lady Gaga wore a dress made out of meat. Today, the dress is in a museum.

Lady Gaga appeared in advertisements for fashion designer Versace.

Fans expect Lady Gaga to wear fun outfits. This makes her a fashion icon.

GIVING BACK

Giving back is important to Lady Gaga. In 2012, she started the Born This Way **Foundation**. This organization teaches people to be kind.

During her free time, Lady Gaga has visited children at homeless shelters. And in 2012, she donated $1 million to help people after Hurricane Sandy hit the East Coast.

FRIENDS OF
THE DALAI LAMA

ci___ __indness.org

In 2016, Lady Gaga met the Dalai Lama (*second from left*). He is the leader of Tibetan Buddhism. His message is to be kind to everyone.

THE SUPER BOWL

The Super Bowl is the largest football game of the year. The **performers** are an important part of the Super Bowl Halftime Show.

Lady Gaga has performed at two Super Bowl games. In 2016, she sang "The Star-Spangled Banner" before the game. The next year, Lady Gaga was the Halftime Show star. More than 111 million people watched her on TV!

During her performance at the 2017 Super Bowl, Lady Gaga flew down from the stadium's ceiling.

BUZZ

Lady Gaga continues to prove she's got limitless potential. In 2018, she will be in a movie called A *Star Is Born*. With Lady Gaga's talent and creativity, fans are excited to see what she'll do next!

Lady Gaga performed with a band called Metallica at the 2017 Grammy Awards.

GLOSSARY

Academy Award an award given by the Academy of Motion Picture Arts and Sciences to the best actors and filmmakers of the year.

advertisement (ad-vuhr-TEYZE-muhnt) a short message in print or on television or radio that helps sell a product.

American Music Award any of the awards given each year by Billboard Magazine and on Billboard.com, based on album and digital singles sales, radio airplay, streaming, social activity and touring.

award something that is given in recognition of good work or a good act.

foundation (faun-DAY-shuhn) an organization that controls gifts of money and services.

Golden Globe Award any of the awards given each year by the Hollywood Foreign Press Association. Golden Globe Awards honor the year's best accomplishments in TV shows and movies.

Grammy Award any of the awards given each year by the National Academy of Recording Arts and Sciences. Grammy Awards honor the year's best accomplishments in music.

jazz a form of American music that features lively and unusual beats. It first became popular in the early 1900s.

nominate to name as a possible winner. A nominee is someone who is nominated.

perform to do something in front of an audience. A performer is someone who performs.

pop relating to popular music.

producer a person who oversees the making of a movie, a play, an album, or a radio or television show.

release to make available to the public.

role a part an actor plays.

WEBSITES

To learn more about Pop Biographies, visit **abdobooklinks.com**. These links are routinely monitored and updated to provide the most current information available.

INDEX